LEE

ALEXANDER

MCQUEEN

Tom Rasmussen

Illustrated by Angie Réhe

LEE

ALEXANDER

MCQUEEN

The Illustrated World of a Fashion Visionary

Smith Street Books

Contents

Lee Alexander McQueen was, and remains, one of the greatest fashion designers the world has ever seen. In his relatively short career, McQueen – like all the design greats – pushed the boundaries of fashion, transforming the industry. He melded fashion and technology, he challenged his audiences, he found beauty in the most unexpected of places, and all the while he made the world watch.

On the eve of 'Plato's Atlantis', his final show before his death, his producer tried on the famous Armadillo boots – the 10-inch heels that became a signature shape for the McQueen brand – and she couldn't walk. She ran to find Lee and explained the problem, worried about the models. He simply replied, 'If they fall, they fall.'

Nobody fell. His producer, Sam Gainsbury, later told *The Guardian*: 'Before the show Lee was backstage with all these seventeen-year-old models, looking into their eyes, telling them how incredible they looked, how proud he was [of them], that they could do it. He gave them such confidence. And not one of them fell. It was like a gift, with Lee. He made you feel like you were capable of anything.'

Featuring an appearance from Lady Gaga, who premiered her new single, the instantly iconic 'Bad Romance', during the show, 'Plato's Atlantis' was the first runway show ever to be streamed live from the catwalk. Instead of going down in history as a tale of tumbling models, it became known as fashion's vision of the future – both in terms of the printed, intricately constructed reptilian garments, and in its depiction of how fashion and technology could work together to expand fashion's audience. Suddenly, the exclusive world of fashion wasn't just for those who had a front-row seat – everyone was invited.

Now, we see this phenomenon everywhere – the democratisation of the catwalk, some might call it – allowing people who had never before had access to a fashion show the chance to get up close and personal to what was happening on the runway. And it was McQueen's boldness in questioning what fashion should be, and who it should be for, that brought about this industry-altering shift.

That's how he approached fashion – as though it was capable of anything. Countless testimonies exist, from those who worked closely with McQueen to those who met him once, all describing his optimism when it came to design: there was nothing that wasn't possible, and McQueen proved this on the runway time and time again.

But beyond his incontestable fashion genius, he was a man full of complexities, living in both darkness and light. He was troubled but sweet, acerbic but deeply loving, an addict, a comedian, a pessimist and an optimist.

While McQueen's designs keep him on the lips and mood-boards of so many people today, his personality, his attitude, and his unlikely position as a working-class boy from East London heralded as the rebel king of fashion, only enhances this legacy – a legacy that is as dark as it is inspiring.

This book is an illustrated view into McQueen's remarkable life and work. It's a celebration of the man and the fashion designer who left fashion, and the world, a little more complex, a little more beautiful, and a little more challenging than he found it.

Youth and

Chapter 1

Education

Lee McQueen was the unlikely trailblazer who changed fashion forever. From a working-class background in East London, McQueen's start in life did not feature glamorous women, high fashion or a focus on art and creativity. Famous for finding beauty in the most unexpected of places, it was at home in the streets of Stratford where McQueen developed his eye for drama, darkness and twisted splendour.

Lee Alexander McQueen, Britain's former reigning king of fashion, was born in Lewisham, East London, on 17 March 1969. The youngest son of Joyce, a school teacher, and Ronald, a taxi driver, McQueen started life in a small council flat, in a block of postwar standard-issue houses, eventually moving to a terraced house in nearby Stratford.

'I always
wanted to be
a designer.
I read books
on fashion
from the age
of 12.'

ALEXANDER MCQUEEN

Less imaginative people would find little inspiration among the brutalist brick and concrete of East London, but McQueen spent his early years gazing at the birds of prey that circled the railway tracks and telephone masts that populate the landscape of East London's industrial heart. These majestic birds, amid their rigid settings, would later come to inform much of McQueen's design aesthetic, and influence his talent for creating beauty from the most meagre and unexpected of things.

In the seventies and eighties, East London wasn't the gentrified creative hub it is now. The streets were much more aggressive, crime was rife, and creativity and flamboyancy weren't met with reward. 'It's an honest place. If someone's gonna mug you they tell you before they do it,' McQueen once remarked. His love of dark beauty was born here, against a backdrop of brown and red brick, and steelwork.

In the early years of his life, Lee shared a small room with his two brothers. Despite his humble beginnings, McQueen had big plans. He announced his dreams of being a fashion designer at a very young age, while attending Carpenters Primary School near his home. He would spend his days draping his sister in bed sheets and curtains he found lying around, making her model for him, bringing to life his first fashion creations.

Known for making garments move, it was here McQueen's eye for draping and skill in manipulating fabric began: at home, his older sister his muse. But for a young boy from a working-class background, these dreams were unlikely to come true. The fashion world is a long way from Stratford, and the elite and nepotistic circles of this milieu can seem impenetrable for those from less-privileged backgrounds.

After primary school, Lee attended Rokeby School in Canning Town, a boys' school where his flamboyant character was often met with homophobic sneers of 'McQueer'. An awkward, imaginative teenager, he struggled to make friends with his classmates.

And while a young McQueen still dreamed of fashion, he left school at sixteen with one qualification in art – an academic record that was unlikely to lead him to the dizzying heights of fashion success. His time at high school remains undiscussed, but like many creative geniuses, McQueen's youth was punctuated with bullying and misunderstanding.

Just after Lee quit school in 1986, he took a course in tailoring at Newham College. His mum saw a news report about the shortage of apprentices skilled enough to work on Savile Row. Knowing he had always been passionate about fashion, she persuaded him to apply for a position assisting London's tailoring masters. His eye for fabric earned him an apprenticeship with Cornelius O'Callaghan on Savile Row – a brilliant coat maker who preferred his assistants to have no fashion training, because that meant they had fewer ideas, and were much easier to train. McQueen was perfect.

The streets of Mayfair are lined by men and women with pockets of gold, and McQueen found himself in the heart of the world's foremost home of fine tailoring, frequented by royalty, aristocracy and the richest subset of the world's population. It was during his first post at the royally appointed tailor Anderson & Sheppard that McQueen imbibed everything there was to know about cutting patterns, tailoring, padding, and building bespoke tailored suits to fit the bodies of the highest-paying customers. Not only was he incredibly skilled, he was also an incredibly quick learner.

Before long, a young McQueen was creating made-to-measure garments for royalty, most notably Prince Charles. Anecdotally, Lee started challenging the status quo by sewing his own brand of subversion into the unseen linings of the garments. 'I'm in Savile Row, at the top of this old building with all these old tailors and it was Prince Charles' jacket I'm working on,' McQueen once explained in a documentary, 'and I draw this big willy on it.' From the word go, Lee's relationship with fashion was one of sabotage and tradition, seeing fashion as a means of expression. Even in a role as prosaic as a tailor on Savile Row, Lee had found a way to subvert the rules and question the hierarchies upon which big institutions are built. Lee would carry this attitude with him throughout his career, and his work would eventually question the very seams upon which fashion and its surrounding industry was sewn.

Meanwhile, Lee's personal life was a far cry from the shining streets of Savile Row. By night, Lee and his friends would flood the streets of Soho, London's gay district. Here was a world that would come to constantly inform McQueen's designs. Full of drugs, poverty, prostitution, sex, alcohol, and night after night of dancing, laughing and loving, Soho was where many of Lee's integral personal relationships would blossom. 'There's always an energy in London: the poverty, the unemployment, the drug-induced environment, the nightlife ...' said Lee. He loved it.

After McQueen completed his apprenticeship at Anderson & Sheppard, he moved two doors down to esteemed tailors Gieves & Hawkes, but swiftly tired of the monotony of tailoring the same thing for the richest of the rich. 'I knew I couldn't survive in a place like that for the rest of my life,' McQueen said. 'Cluttered in a small workshop, padding lapels. But I was good at it: I could tailor a jacket very quickly. I was quick at learning ... And I wanted to learn everything.'

McQueen eventually left Gieves & Hawkes, and moved 'down the Row' – to Bermans & Nathans – where he took up a role in the pattern-cutting department, learning to cut intricate lines in the most expensive fabric.

After his time on Savile Row, a twenty-year-old McQueen moved a little further west – to Notting Hill – to the house of heralded designer Koji Tatsuno, as a pattern cutter. McQueen was in his element for a time: working for the house that was globally famed for taking vintage fabrics and reworking them into contemporary, expressive, exciting women's clothes. But fashions change, as does the revenue a company brings in, and a downsize in the middle of a financial recession saw McQueen made redundant and unsure where to head next.

So, like anyone with fashion nous, he persuaded his sister, a travel agent, to book him a one-way ticket to Milan. 'The biggest thing at that time was Romeo Gigli,' McQueen explained. 'He was everywhere. I thought, this is the only person I want to work for. I was twenty years old. I walked into Romeo Gigli with the worst portfolio you've ever seen, full of costume design. They said they had nothing for me and that they'd call me if anything came up. Anyway, I was walking down the street afterwards and this girl came screaming up to me like a madwoman: "Stop, stop, stop, Romeo wants to see you. He wants to see you tomorrow. Come back."'

Gigli took a shine to Lee, who quickly started pattern cutting for the Milanese house. Some years later, Romeo Gigli would recount a story that captured McQueen's anti-establishment attitude towards rules: when working on a new jacket style for the designer, Lee was asked to remake it three times. After the third try, Gigli took apart the jacket, only to find the words 'Fuck you' scrawled on the inner lining.

McQueen returned to London armed with a technical knowledge that would rival the most skilled makers in the industry. He'd learned the need for precision from Savile Row, complex pattern cutting during a short stint at Bermans & Nathans, expressive construction at Koji Tatsuno, and the importance of pace and perfection at Romeo Gigli. But equally important to all this skill was McQueen's energy, his outlook and his friends.

It was the collision of Lee's impressive technical skill and outrageous personal life that would enable him to create fashion visions nobody had ever imagined possible – McQueen included.

By late 1990 McQueen was twenty-one, broke and out of work. While trawling for jobs in the trade, he saw an ad for a position teaching pattern cutting at the world-renowned art and design school at Central Saint Martins. Bobby Hillson, the Fashion Masters course director at the time, found McQueen loitering outside her door. She asked him what he wanted, and he answered, 'A job.' Bobby knew that the students would never take Lee seriously as he was the same age as them, and didn't give him the job. But she did start to talk to him about the Fashion MA. Fascinated by his energy, she asked him to come back with samples of his tailoring and his drawings.

Hillson later reflected in the documentary *McQueen and I* that she'd thought, 'He probably won't last. He probably won't be able to take it. Because all the others [students] had come up through the right routes.' But, lo and behold, McQueen enrolled in the Fashion MA course at Central Saint Martins, and spent the year impressing his once-dubious teachers.

This was perhaps the biggest turning point in McQueen's life to date. Now, instead of being within the structure of a brand, he was to be the brand – creating his own vision from start to finish. Nobody would be asking him to remake something, to cut it differently, or to avoid profane or subversive references. And, for the first time, against the odds, this working-class young gay man from East London had started making his childhood dreams come true.

As the runway shows for the students' graduate collections rolled around, the fashion press clamoured to see what Central Saint Martins' class of '92 would bring to the fashion forum. For many, this show is the most exposure their work will ever get, but McQueen's graduate runway set him on a direct path to stardom. The extraordinary Isabella Blow, contributing fashion stylist at *Vogue* magazine, was looking on from the steps of the venue. Blow was fashion dynamite, and she would go on to become McQueen's biggest champion.

'The pieces went past me, and they moved in a way I'd never seen,' Blow remarked of Lee's graduate collection, entitled 'Jack the Ripper Stalks His Victims', in which long silk coats in pink, black and red fluttered down the runway. Each piece had a lock of McQueen's hair bonded between two pieces of acrylic on the inside: representing the old tradition of giving hair to a lover as a token, often purchased from prostitutes rather than cut from their own hair.

Little did Blow or McQueen know that their meeting would change both of their lives irrevocably. Blow was smitten with the collection, calling and calling McQueen's home phone from her office at *Vogue*. After almost twenty phone calls, McQueen finally returned one. There and then she offered him £5000 for his entire graduate collection. He said yes.

The
Collections

Chapter 2

1992–97

McQueen's runway shows for his self-titled brand were where his imagination really came to life. This was where he redefined the limits of what fashion could be, and snatched the attention of both the fashion industry and the world. From blood to urine, birds of prey to earthworms, McQueen's daring, often outrageous approach to runway shows catapulted him to global fame and commercial success, and cemented his position as one of the most influential fashion designers in history.

Spanning three major cities, McQueen's collections grew in style and scale over his twenty-year career, and his runway shows never failed to stimulate, challenge and shock their viewers. Tickets to a McQueen show were like gold dust, with editors, fashion press and obsessive fans and clients alike desperate to be part of the next glorious, controversial frontier. Whatever McQueen's chosen context, he was truly momentous. 'Give me time and I'll give you a revolution,' he once said. And he was right: he revolutionised fashion over and over again.

'I think there is beauty in everything. What "normal" people would perceive as ugly, I can usually see something of beauty in it.'

ALEXANDER MCQUEEN

MA GRADUATE COLLECTION 1992
'Jack the Ripper Stalks His Victims'

McQueen's use of darkness in his designs revealed itself very early on. In his graduate collection, he was inspired by Jack the Ripper, the East London killer who stalked and murdered prostitutes during the 1880s. McQueen grew up not far from the site of the murders – it was rumoured that a relative of his rented a room to one of the Ripper's victims. The collection itself is the stuff of fashion legend now, with only a few pieces still in existence. It featured tailored coats in dark fabrics and giant skirts with faces printed across them, and mixed old English Victoriana with a sexual energy that was rare on the runway at the time. The most famous piece is perhaps a pink silk tail coat, covered in printed thorns.

AUTUMN/WINTER 1993
'Taxi Driver'

In the history of fashion, there have been very few designers who could lay claim to inventing a brand-new silhouette. But McQueen, in his second-ever collection, had done just that. Apparently inspired by the builder's bum, the Bumster was tailored perfectly to bisect the body at the exact halfway point: a line on the body that had never been explored before. The only person known to own an original pair of Bumsters is the iconic princess of pop, Kylie Minogue, who ordered a pair directly from McQueen. The rest of the collection, inspired by the gritty, bloody movie *Taxi Driver*, was left in trash bags outside a club on the night of the show. The trash bags were disposed of by street cleaners while McQueen partied inside, oblivious, until the early hours of the morning.

SPRING/SUMMER 1994
'Nihilism'

This was McQueen's big London Fashion debut and first professional catwalk show. No longer a student, this moment would be make or break for Lee. Nihilism, in philosophical terms, means 'the belief that nothing in the world has a real existence'. Take that further into psychology, and nihilism speaks of a body and a mind that don't exist, that don't matter. Gathered in a market building in South London, McQueen showed the world his nihilistic viewpoint through his use of translucent fabrics and silhouettes, which obscured, but never blocked, the wearer. Some pieces were made of cellophane, while zips were rusted and outfits spattered with what looked like dried blood. McQueen, from the off, was comfortable with darkness and the macabre – and while the clothes were fresh and to this day appear forward-thinking, the ideas McQueen was already playing with in his first collection post graduation would set the stage for a career and a life that toyed with both great meaning and deep nihilism.

AUTUMN/WINTER 1994
'Banshee'

The location: legendary London nightclub, Café de Paris.
McQueen's clothes had just been shot for the racy new
magazine *Dazed & Confused*, and Isabella Blow was now
proudly championing this *enfant terrible* of the London
scene. The whole fashion crowd turned out for McQueen's
second professional show out of fashion school (unheard
of!). They watched in delight as sharp tailoring, plaster
bustiers and knitwear with holes at the breasts marched
their way down the runway in an ode to the Irish folkloric
idea of the banshee: women who could be heard wailing
as boats sank at sea. McQueen was starting to play with
romance, with beauty, with the gothic. Reviews read that
this was a departure from his previous collection, which had
been deemed brilliant but angry. Now we were starting to
see a little more softness … and London loved it.

SPRING/SUMMER 1995
'The Birds'

Ever inspired by birds, McQueen's collection featured what would become his signature swallow print, which lives on across his designs even today. Featuring models including a young *Vogue* editor, Plum Sykes, and the remarkably contorted, corseted Mr Pearl with his tiny cinched waist, 'The Birds' was the collection where McQueen first introduced what would eventually become the fashion house's DNA: deconstructed tailoring.

AUTUMN/WINTER 1995
'Highland Rape'

Always delving into history, this time exploring his Scottish heritage, 'Highland Rape' became one of McQueen's most criticised and adored collections. With some of the press branding it misogynistic and fetishising of violence against women, others felt it was deeply emotional and a commentary on the way women's bodies were used in warfare.

Suzy Menkes said that this was the first time she'd ever seen McQueen truly put himself into his work, and the result was astounding. Women with torn tartan dresses stumbled across the runway in a collection inspired by the ethnic cleansing of Scottish Highland natives by British forces in the eighteenth and nineteenth centuries. For this collection, McQueen revisited the Bumster, and tailored dresses so they would drape and fall from each model's frame perfectly and precisely.

'My work is not about being shocking, but about putting yourself in danger.'

ALEXANDER MCQUEEN

SPRING/SUMMER 1996
'The Hunger'

Worms. In fashion. Actual worms, in fashion. Yes, of course that was McQueen. Referencing the erotic vampire movie *The Hunger*, models famously flipped off the audience while wearing bondage straps and perspex corsets that sealed live worms and long hairs inside them. The models were often dripping with blood and wearing casts, all while donning precisely cut and constructed tailored jackets and skin-tight pencil skirts.

AUTUMN/WINTER 1996
'Dante'

Always looking for the next way to shock the press, McQueen cheekily sat a skeleton in the front row for the show. Noted editors and fashion folk were greeted by the skeleton as they filed into a candlelit church in East London's Spitalfields, McQueen's chosen setting for the next of his dramatic instalments. It was in 'Dante' that Lee began to explore religious signifiers and Victoriana, an aesthetic that became a major building block in the brand's DNA. Blasphemy, beauty, brilliance.

SPRING/SUMMER 1997
'Bellmer La Poupée'

One of Lee's most talked about and most controversial
shows remains 1997's 'Bellmer La Poupée'. An ode to
photographer Hans Bellmer and his rearranged dolls,
McQueen sent models down a watery runway encumbered
by various metal structures. Tailoring – yes, and the Bumster
on his dear friend Kate Moss. With clean lines and plenty of
looks in a single fabric, for 'La Poupée' McQueen contorted,
elongated and distorted the silhouette, whether through the
cut of a pant or the giant metal square strapped to the legs
and arms of a model. Most comfortable with discomfort,
this felt like both modernity and archaism: women who were
sexy, technologically advanced, walking on water even,
and yet still restricted in violent and uncomfortable ways by
absurd metal structures. Of his famous Bumster, McQueen
said: 'I wanted to elongate the body, not just show the bum.
To me, that part of the body – not so much the buttocks,
but the bottom of the spine – that's the most erotic part of
anyone's body, man or woman.'

Alexander

Chapter 3

and Issie

Lee McQueen and Isabella Blow formed the world's most renowned fashion friendship. Issie dubbed him Alexander, and Alexander brought Issie's fashion dreams to life. Together, the pair were prolific, their relationship tumultuous, and their legacy tremendous.

Isabella Blow was one of fashion's last true eccentrics. She was known in the fashion community for her true lust for style, and for her utter dedication to living a life surrounded by beauty. In McQueen, Isabella found boundless beauty in the most unlikely of places: a chubby, working-class lad from East London.

'He's a wild bird with a good silhouette. Birds have movement, they have freedom, they're wild, they're free. They don't have to be responsible to anyone except their great technical ability to fly. And he makes clothes fly.'

ISABELLA BLOW

It was love at first sight. In February 1992, when Blow failed to get a seat at McQueen's virtuoso Saint Martins' graduate show, she opted for a seat on the floor instead. Issie became obsessed. She was so drawn by the darkness, the 'flesh and blood' in McQueen's graduate collection that she was determined to buy the entire collection outright before anyone else could. 'The next day I rang up, and I couldn't get hold of him,' Blow explained. 'His mother said to Alexander, "There's this madwoman who keeps trying to call us. She wants some of your clothes." I rang between six and eight times a day. Finally, I got a little voice at the end of the line.'

That little voice was McQueen's, and he agreed to sell Blow the collection. In the true style of English aristocrats, she was dead broke, so each week Blow and McQueen would stop at different ATMs across London, where she would withdraw £100 in return for a black bin bag full of pieces from McQueen's collection. Already confident in his skill, McQueen wouldn't haggle, and the pair continued this 'buy now pay later' scheme until Blow had coughed up the promised £5000.

This sealed their relationship. In Issie, Lee had found an unlikely muse, his first patron, and his biggest champion. And in Lee, Issie had found someone to nurture, to mother and to influence.

Together, the pair took the fashion industry by storm. It was like an explosion: rock met roll, and everyone was hooked. McQueen's designs and Blow's attitude both possessed a rawness that was perfect for fashion at the time. It caused shock and dismay across the world, but it kept people coming back, time after time, to witness the next spectacle. Blow once described fashion as sabotage and tradition, and both Blow and McQueen utterly personified this.

Soon it was time for McQueen's first post-graduation collection, a gritty, blood-splattered homage to the brilliant movie *Taxi Driver*. For this next show, McQueen was one of six designers invited by the British Fashion Council to exhibit at The Ritz hotel. Blow and McQueen had become a fashion force, and stories later surfaced of how Blow tore through the corridors of The Ritz, dragging all her fashion friends to the showroom to lay eyes on the 'next big thing'. And boy, was she right.

'The pieces went past me and they moved in a way I had never seen and I wanted them. I just knew he had something really special, very modern, it was about sabotage and tradition.'

ISABELLA BLOW

By this time, McQueen had undergone perhaps his most important rebranding: changing his name from Lee to Alexander – his middle name. 'Everyone else calls him Lee. I call him Alexander, because of Alexander the Great,' was Isabella's reasoning. In McQueen she had found a platonic soulmate, a person she could support and encourage. She offered him access to all manner of things, from her country house to her little black book of big fashion contacts.

'He was chubby, smiley, beautiful,' Issie once said of McQueen. Blow would invite McQueen to go to her country pile, Hilles, where she lived with her husband, Detmar. During downtime, Blow ensured McQueen had plenty to keep him occupied. She would organise lavish dinners, and falconry lessons with birds like those McQueen grew up watching – but these ones responded to his call and came to his wrist.

Blow's glorious country manor would become a home away from home for an increasingly successful McQueen, a kind of den of delights and revelry. Issie and McQueen were close friends for over fifteen years, and at Hilles the pair spent countless nights drinking, taking drugs and talking into the small hours, until McQueen eventually retired to the palatial Long Room, reserved for Blow's esteemed guests. McQueen would go to Hilles for extended periods: to rest, to work, to escape London or Paris, to shoot clay pigeons, to simply look to nature for inspiration.

Issie's influence, however, went deeper than just extravagant pleasures and countryside inspirations, extending to brilliant contacts and remarkable press coverage, which helped McQueen achieve unprecedented industry success very early on. Within the first few years of McQueen's career, Blow had featured his work in a giant spread in *The Face* magazine, and had also modelled for *Vogue* wearing head-to-toe McQueen. This was an accolade unheard of for a designer just starting out. But Blow adored McQueen like her own child – and she loved his clothes even more.

At every McQueen show, there were always two people who stood up the whole time in utter joy and support for Lee: his mum and Issie. Even when McQueen eventually took the reins at the storied Parisian fashion house Givenchy, which caused bad blood with Blow, she still sat front row and applauded every look that came down the runway.

Within three years of meeting the pair had conquered London and initiated a brand-new wave of brilliant Britannia. The world began looking to London for innovative, exciting answers to fashion's questions. This period is still known as one of the most riveting times in fashion, a period people often try to replicate, although nobody has succeeded yet.

Their relationship was constantly being reimagined in new formats: Isabella as muse, confidante, patron, mother and press manager. For McQueen's 1994 show 'Banshee', Blow even offered herself up as a model. Held at the once-iconic Café de Paris in London's Piccadilly, the unlikely model graced the runway in a lace dress, waistcoat and a high-collared shirt in a regal purple. Issie's hair was lacquered flat to her face, and McQueen's surname was intricately lettered across her idiosyncratic jet-black bob in bright silver. Issie's turn on the runway was met with cheers and applause from her many friends and admirers, and when she appeared in her second outfit she famously paused and took another lap around the runway, loving every moment.

Stories like these populate the colourful, outrageous, absurd history of fashion's favourite friendship. Now that the gates to the fashion collective had been smashed open by McQueen with Issie at his side, the industry became populated with a far more diverse crowd. The misfits had risen to power, and fast.

In 1997, Givenchy were seeking a new creative director to replace John Galliano. By then, McQueen had gained such momentum he'd become a hurricane. And so, just six years after presenting his graduate collection, he was the only option for Givenchy. A post usually taken by a master was now filled by a rebel.

This was it! McQueen was, once again, on the up, and perhaps now his number one supporter and muse, after a much longer life in fashion, would finally be rewarded with a well-paid position and, most importantly, a true creative role in making fashion. When the contracts were signed with Givenchy, the pair celebrated over caviar and champagne. But to Issie's dismay, she was nowhere to be seen in the deal. In a move that shocked both the industry and Issie herself, Lee had purposefully omitted her and left Issie to hear of her exclusion from others. Many said that the friendship never quite recovered. Issie took herself back to London, heartbroken and betrayed, while McQueen set up shop in the Givenchy studios in Paris.

According to her husband, Detmar, Issie was devastated, 'But the problem was Issie couldn't fall out with him because she was addicted to McQueen. She didn't want to lose the clothes.' Instead, Blow did everything she could to support McQueen in his new role – organising shoots with prestigious photographers and models; trying to claim a €35,000 Givenchy dress as an expense on her business account at *The Sunday Times*; applauding every single look on the runway at McQueen's 'disastrous' first Givenchy show. She even turned up to one of McQueen's shows in a full dog suit and collar in the hope that he'd like it. But by 1998, even Issie had realised the changing stakes of their relationship. 'It's like vampires ... you need somebody and then you don't need the drug anymore,' she once said of McQueen's treatment of her.

While McQueen's tenure at Givenchy slowly began to blossom, Blow's journalistic career was also resuscitated after she was reappointed to her former fashion position at *Tatler*. For a few years, their paths were smooth, though they crossed less and less in the wake of one of fashion's most shocking betrayals.

A few years passed, by which time the pair shared much love but little creative collaboration. And while there was endless speculation about whether the infamous duo really cared for each other, when Blow was admitted to rehab in 2006, McQueen – who was by now incredibly well off – paid most of the fee, desperate for her to overcome the depression she had been battling for years. Having separated from Detmar, Isabella completed her treatment and went back to Hilles to make peace with her husband. But McQueen, by this point, disapproved of Isabella's relationship with Detmar, and the pair drifted apart once again.

On 6 May 2007, the much-adored, respected and revered Isabella Blow swallowed weed-killer at her home in Gloucestershire and subsequently passed away in Gloucestershire Royal Hospital the following day. 'I'm fighting depression, and I can't beat it,' Blow told her husband, Detmar. Like so many brilliant artists before her, Isabella's depression won a lifelong battle. But Blow's legacy – from the talent she discovered to the way she lived, dressed, and revelled in life – will forever live on.

McQueen never really recovered from losing Issie, one of the
great loves of his life. Five months after her passing, McQueen
and Philip Treacy – another of Blow's protégés – staged 'Le Dame
Bleue' in Paris: a fashion show in memory of one of the few true
icons fashion ever knew. Even in her death, she remained at the
heart of McQueen's work. Journalists and editors concurred that
the show was one of the most powerful, meaningful moments
fashion has ever seen, with many observing that such moments
transcend fashion entirely. Together, McQueen and Blow
were the pair who dedicated their lives to achieving just that:
transcending fashion.

'A muse is someone who is a constant inspiration,' Blow said of
her relationship with McQueen. 'You can't buy a muse, it's like a
love affair with somebody.' And for McQueen and Blow, however
tumultuous their relationship, it really, really was.

The
Collections

Chapter 4

1997–2001

The never-ending buzz generated by his collections made McQueen one of the first real rockstars of the fashion design world. Gone were the days of the silent genius, locked in a studio, sending demure messages through only their clothes. Although this attitude still played a huge part in McQueen's process, he had quickly risen to the top, becoming the commander-in-chief of what was cool. A rockstar, a celebrity in his own right.

People were desperate for his work, and for the rebellious status that came with it. The nineties were in full swing, and European club culture, cheap travel and cheap drugs were taking all industries to new heights. With the internet slowly starting to make sense, communication was quicker, and the closed walls of industries like fashion were being brought down by the likes of McQueen and his misfits – proving to onlookers that even the most unlikely could enter the fashion arena.

It was an exciting and bold move for the iconic Parisienne couture house Givenchy to welcome McQueen – who had graduated from university a mere six years previously – as their creative director. Until then, appointments like this simply didn't happen. And, in true McQueen style, he rose to the prestigious opportunity in the best way he knew how: with outrage and rebellion. There are endless accounts of McQueen swanning into the Givenchy atelier in Paris, taking designs that skilled craftsmen and women had worked on for weeks, and chopping them up on the mannequin in front of everyone. He caused utter dismay among the French press – who laud and protect their native design talents – after telling one journalist he thought Hubert de Givenchy, the house's founder, had no talent.

He was set for stardom. But as his first Givenchy show 'Search for the Golden Fleece' rolled around, McQueen learned what it was to fail. Journalists, editors and faithful clients felt McQueen's first offering in the couture arena was superficial, poorly thought out and gimmicky. In hindsight, McQueen thought so too, admitting in an interview that this first collection was 'crap'.

Lee remained at Givenchy for four years, while still producing his shows for his own Alexander McQueen label, happily making a profit for Givenchy with his subsequent collections. It became evident over the time he was there that his energies were better spent on his home turf in London, where his eponymous brand had continued to flourish. After his first collection at Givenchy, McQueen had begun to play ball, incorporating the traditional house codes into collections that he aimed at a younger clientele. But it was at his Alexander McQueen label, less penned in by rules and regulations, that McQueen produced radical collections like 'Joan', 'The Overlook' and 'Eye' – and where people still got their true McQueen fix.

In 2000, when the Gucci group appointed designer Tom Ford to invest in fashion houses around the world, top of his list was Alexander McQueen. Within months the deal was done, and McQueen had sold 51 per cent of his company to the global giant – and the main competitor of LVMH, who owned Givenchy.

While French houses have always favoured the brilliance of British designers, they've never shied away from cutting ties to them, either – as evidenced in the termination of McQueen's tenure at Givenchy after news of the Gucci deal broke. His final show at Givenchy was stripped of its production, and shown in two quiet sittings to a select group of editors and buyers totalling less than ninety people.

Even though McQueen's time at Givenchy is often seen as a side-note in his creative archive, it had brought him to a global audience – an audience that followed him back to London, where he now had more budget, more production, and more vigour than ever. It was the millennium, and a new dawn for McQueen.

'You can only go forward by making mistakes. I'm 27, not 57. I'm not Givenchy, I'm Alexander McQueen.'

ALEXANDER MCQUEEN

AUTUMN/WINTER 1997
'It's a Jungle Out There'

Hair became manes, eyes became slicked with thick
black eyeliner; feral models stormed the butcher's station
at Borough Market, which, back then, was a real, gritty
London trade market – a shock for the tottering editors in
attendance. Inspired by HG Wells' infamous novel, *The Island
of Doctor Moreau*, McQueen played a fashion vivisectionist:
slicing and stitching animal skins, patched here and there
to create models of half-animal, half-human appearance.
Kate Moss tore down the runway like a wild predator, while
audience members reportedly fainted at the overwhelming
beastliness of fashion's most beautiful girls.

SPRING/SUMMER 1998
'The Golden Shower'/'Untitled'

While McQueen was primarily focused on exploring pain, he knew better than most just how closely pain links with pleasure. The collection's tailoring started sharp, slowly growing looser and sheerer, exposing flesh as the show went on. In the second half, golden rain fell from above, soaking the models through and exposing naked skin beneath sheer white outfits. Originally named 'The Golden Shower' – after the act of urination during sex – corporate sponsors were apparently outraged at the unadulterated sexuality of the show, and demanded a name change. Now the collection is known as 'Untitled', but who can forget a golden shower?

AUTUMN/WINTER 1998
'Joan'

For autumn, McQueen wanted to warm up. Moving on from cold, golden rain, this season the designer played with fire – literally. Layer upon layer of metal mesh was printed with the faces of the Romanov children. Models wore bald caps and red contact lenses. Flowing gowns were juxtaposed against dramatic red python-print fabric; some models even walked in chainmail. The finale, perhaps one of McQueen's most memorable scenes, saw a model in all red encircled in flames – a reference to the Catholic martyr and feminist hero Joan of Arc. As the flames grew, so did the volume of Diana Ross's voice, bursting with the lyrics 'you're gonna make it, you're gonna make it' over an iconic disco beat.

SPRING/SUMMER 1999
'No. 13'

On the brink of the millennium, the world was asking questions about its relationship with technology: what was coming, what had passed. In an empty warehouse usually used to house street-cleaning trucks, McQueen was about to create one of fashion's most remembered and revered moments. The show started with a nod to the Edwardian Arts and Crafts movement, which favoured traditional craftsmanship over machine-made products – materials featured included leather, wood and intricate lacework. Dramatically curved articulated winged bodices soared. Aimee Mullins, the para-athlete beloved by McQueen, walked the show with carved wooden prosthetic legs. As the show reached a climax, the legendary Shalom Harlow stalked to the centre of the warehouse in a white paper gown. There, she spun round and round on a turntable as two robotic arms spray-painted her dress and skin with black and neon-yellow paint. It was the tension point between past and future – the detail and human skill of the handmade in combat with the aggression and mechanisation of technology. It is to this day seen as one of McQueen's – and fashion's – most jaw-dropping and pivotal shows. It predicted, as so many of McQueen's shows did, a frustrating and complex battle for power between people and technology managing to act of its own free will. Onlookers were reportedly deeply shocked and deeply moved. McQueen at his best.

i

AUTUMN/WINTER 1999
'The Overlook'

Inspired by classic horror films, 'The Overlook' took reference from *The Shining*, but with a twist. Many argue this show was one of McQueen's most poetic, staged in an enormous lucite snow globe, with giant shearling coats, huge hand knits and intricate patchworking. Ice skaters peppered the Victorian scene. This was emblematic of McQueen's most important skills: to dream up shows of pure beauty, featuring clothes that were, ultimately, wearable and sellable. This was McQueen's genius formula, which so few before or after him could achieve.

SPRING/SUMMER 2000
'Eye'

McQueen moved stateside for his first collection post the turn of the millennium. The whole fashion industry trekked far from the centre of Manhattan, to a huge warehouse on the West Side pier, to witness what genius McQueen might dream up in this new American context. As ever, it was drama from start to finish. Models waded through what appeared to be black water, in a show that mixed sportswear, sex and Middle Eastern references. The show featured a powerhouse Gisele Bündchen in an embroidered head covering and metal bodysuit, stomping down the runway, all-powerful in McQueen's creations. Slowly, spikes rose through the water, setting the audience on the edge of their seats as acrobats dangled above thousands of sharp metal points, performing dances in red and black burqa-like outfits. Ever the showman, the runway presentation climaxed with McQueen dropping his trousers, revealing boxer shorts plastered with stars and stripes.

AUTUMN/WINTER 2000
'Eshu'

Back to London and McQueen's favoured theme of
Victoriana, this time married with Nigerian influence.
Björk would begin her long-term artistic relationship with
the designer here, going on to be photographed in an acid-
washed hoop dress that was very in sync with the trends
of the noughties. Eshu was a Yoruba spirit, a messenger
between heaven and earth. And McQueen sent angels
down the runway: white leathers, leg-of-mutton sleeves,
heads leaved with gold. Bodices were moulded to the body,
brown leather was patched onto coats and pulled around
the body. Denim – jeans and skirts, both flared – was a
heavy feature, as well as natural cottons made hard with
what appeared to be red clay. Lemon yellow, black,
brown and cream formed the limited colour palette of
the collection. As the show continued, models began
to appear with what might be described as loosely 'tribal'
jewellery, although not typically linked to the Yoruba. This
collection, then and now, felt like a heavy-handed attempt
to take inspiration from a culture that McQueen clearly
didn't understand. The clothes were beautiful, but the
show missed the mark.

SPRING/SUMMER 2001
'Voss'

If any show cemented McQueen as the king of fashion theatre, it was 'Voss'. A truly monumental work in McQueen's oeuvre, attendees were seated in a mirrored box, staring at their own reflections for nearly an hour before the show began. The lights flickered on, revealing the insides of this enclosure: a psychiatric ward of sorts, housing yet another box in the centre. Models flitted through the doors and into the space, writhing and squirming, wearing tops made of jigsaw pieces, epaulettes replaced by stuffed rats, and headpieces holding flying taxidermy eagles. It was mania, underpinned by utterly breathtaking clothes that featured embroidered castles, pearlescent party dresses and tailored pantsuits. When the show was seemingly over, the PA blared with the sound of heavy breathing. Models scratched at the windows of the show space, and the four walls of the central box fell to the floor, shattering on impact and revealing a naked Michelle Olley – a performance artist – breathing through tubes and covered in moths that flew free over McQueen's latest creation. The question of whether fashion can ever be art was put to rest that day, as McQueen transcended the role of clothing designer, firmly placing himself among many of the world's greatest contemporary artists.

AUTUMN/WINTER 2001
'What a Merry-Go-Round'

This was McQueen's final show at the Gatliff Warehouse, which had become the setting for so many of his previous shows. It was a show of both dreams and nightmares: upon arrival a colourful merry-go-round lit the space, evoking childhood memories of good times spent at the seaside. But, of course, as the lights went down McQueen's twisted tale sprung to life. Models pole-danced and gyrated on the scene, in denims, PVC and S&M-style pieces, while a backdrop revealed discarded dolls and stuffed toys. Was McQueen reckoning with a lost youth, commenting on the dark circus that fashion can so quickly become, or simply working to shock? Likely a mixture of all three.

McQueen

Chapter 5

the Man

McQueen's star had risen. While he was lauded publicly as a fashion genius, behind closed doors McQueen was gentle, cheeky and hardworking. Surrounded by a team of brilliant women, incredibly close with his mum, and with a love for escaping to the depths of the seas and the expansive English countryside, McQueen's life outside of fashion shaped what he showed within it. Away from the public eye, however, McQueen battled with addiction and depression, and despite his success eventually took his own life. His is a story of brilliance and tragedy, and while he is remembered for his influence on fashion, he was known to friends and family as a loving, caring, irreplaceable man.

By the millennium, Alexander McQueen was one of the most well-known, loved and revered designers the fashion industry, and the world, had ever known. This chubby lad from East London had shown the world the darkest, most brilliant depths of his mind, and proven that fashion could be a radical arena for conversation, politics and art.

'I didn't plan out my life like that. When people recognise and respect what you do, that's nice, but I don't think you ever do this to be famous. Fame should be left to the film stars. We're just offering a service.'

ALEXANDER MCQUEEN

In 2003, he was named International Designer of the Year, British Designer of the Year – an award he received four times – and was awarded a CBE by Queen Elizabeth II for his contribution to the world of fashion. Just eleven years after he graduated from Central Saint Martins and established a whirlwind friendship with Isabella Blow, McQueen had solidified his position as a true fashion icon.

After shirking his father's expectations that he go into a trade, McQueen went on to stage a brilliant takeover of the global fashion industry. This one man can be credited not only with changing the realm of design during his reign as the Rebel King, but also with shaping today's fashion industry in its embrace of technology, its sociopolitical edge, and its democratisation into a global obsession rather than an elitist profession for a chosen few.

Yet while McQueen was forever stretching and twisting the puppet strings, smashing the limits and offering fashion a view of its own potential, his personal life was left largely undiscussed. In order to create such change in an industry obsessed with itself, McQueen had to be drawing his influences from somewhere outside of fashion. And indeed he was.

In the early days – as Lee changed to Alexander, and his collections began to make waves across the world – he was exactly the same boy who'd grown up misunderstood, anti-establishment, and always challenging his critics through shock. It was the time of new rave. Ecstasy had just become available and was rip-roaring through the London nightlife scene like no drug had before. It changed music, partying, everything, and – as orchestrated by McQueen – this new age of partying changed fashion, too.

While McQueen's days were spent in his small studio in Hoxton, East London – a hub of cheap property and high creativity at the time – his nights were spent with his friends in London's gay heart: Soho. Populated by prostitutes, drag queens, flamboyant gay men and butch lesbians, McQueen's evenings were often whiled away in the glorious, nihilistic world of gay clubbing, cigarette smoke, drugs and dancing.

It was on these streets that McQueen found a group of misfits with whom he perfectly fit. They would come to his shows and help in the preceding chaos, all sewing, styling and smoking to the last minute. His mum, Joyce, would arrive with sandwiches for everyone as they worked to produce Lee's early masterpieces. It was thrilling, energetic, and like nothing fashion had ever seen.

'I don't want to do a cocktail party. I'd rather people left my show and vomited. I prefer extreme reactions. I want heart attacks. I want ambulances.'

ALEXANDER MCQUEEN

By the mid-nineties, McQueen was spending less time with this set, although they still received much of his adoration, as well as some fantastic free clothes. As he rocketed to fashion fame, he found himself spending most of his time with his friend and on-and-off muse, Isabella Blow, at her country estate, Hilles, in Gloucestershire. Here, Isabella offered him lessons in falconry. As a teenager, McQueen had been a keen birdwatcher, and an active member of his high school's ornithologists' club.

McQueen's work in fashion constantly referenced the birds he loved, from his early collection, 'The Birds', to the falcon headdresses seen at 'Voss', to the famous Birds of Paradise dress. Even today, McQueen's take on the swallow forms the central logo of his diffusion line, McQ. Across his career, fashion critics would continue to admire the freedom of movement in his work, a skill McQueen had witnessed in the birds he so adoringly watched over the years.

While McQueen was receiving accolades – and creating outrage – for his fashions, he attracted a set of famous friends. Within a few years he had gone from working for others to working for himself, and had become a leader in his field. He was a favourite of the supers of the nineties – Kate Moss, Sophie Dahl and Naomi Campbell all adored him, eventually becoming close friends outside of the fashion game.

By 1997 McQueen was designing tour costumes for none other than David Bowie. He designed Bowie's entire wardrobe for his 1997 tour, as well as the famed Union Jack jacket, immortalised on the cover of the pop legend's twentieth album, *Earthling*.

Before long, the singer Björk had recognised McQueen's talents. His designs featured on the cover of her 1997 album *Homogenic*, lensed by the legendary Nick Knight, who would become one of McQueen's biggest collaborators. McQueen directed the video for 'Alarm Call', from the same album (also shot by Knight). A trippy journey through a rainforest river, Björk rafts through vertical bodies of water and grasps for beams of sunlight, her McQueen dress eventually being feasted on by piranhas.

Yet while McQueen's falling in with the in-crowd was the beginning of many beautiful friendships, as well as genius artistic collaborations, people later reported that his unbridled success changed him. Coming from a place with little money to having an expense account and a high income, he would readily spend thousands of pounds shopping, and often consumed copious amounts of drugs just to keep himself going.

Despite this, he always retained a close, loving relationship with his mother, whom he utterly adored. They were a hilarious double act, bickering and smoking on the sidelines of shows. Although his relationship with other family members was somewhat tumultuous, Joyce was always there, looking on with pride at every show. Interviewed by Joyce for *The Guardian*, in 2004, she asked him what makes him proud. He replied, 'You.'

His beloved dogs were another source of grounding among all the success. McQueen's three pet English bull terriers were like children to him – he absolutely adored them, taking them everywhere. They were rumoured to sleep on Roberto Cavalli cushions. There are countless stories of the dogs bounding about backstage at every show, with McQueen even bringing two of them onto the runway for his bow after one show.

By the time McQueen joined Givenchy in 1997, he was designing four, sometimes six collections a year. These collections were of an epic scale, and with the world watching his every move – both at Givenchy and at McQueen – each collection, with his growing success, held higher stakes than the last. But McQueen rose to the challenge time and again, harnessing the evidently expansive limits of his imagination and producing acclaimed collection after acclaimed collection that shocked the press and had the world hooked. He made fashion exciting again, invigorating both fashion and its followers with brand-new perspectives.

These perspectives came from everything around him. McQueen was also an obsessive film fan. Looking across his collections, you can spot countless references to the cinematic greats. His second collection was inspired by the blood and dirt of Martin Scorsese's iconic *Taxi Driver*. A 2005 collection was based on *Picnic at Hanging Rock*, directed by Peter Weir, and 'The Overlook' in 1999 aimed to find a softer side to Kubrick's chilling *The Shining*.

He was obsessed with historical texts, and adored iconic religious imagery. He took inspiration from places completely outside fashion, often looking at how a time or cultural context would treat its women. From asylums to Joan of Arc, from Jack the Ripper to the Highland Clearances, his work was not just about history, religion or iconography, but about the women inside those things. He was a master at marrying unlikely references – often the historic with the contemporary – and translating them into mind-blowing shows filled to the brim with wearable pieces that still seemed to narrate something new about modern society.

Behind McQueen was a team of dedicated women who helped him realise his wild ideas. Katy England, the silent hero of McQueen's great creative success, met him outside his second-ever runway show. They instantly clicked and would go on to work together for over a decade. From the first show she styled – 'The Birds' in 1995 – to when she resigned as creative director of the McQueen brand in 2007, she was his confidante, second opinion, and his fit model on whom he'd try all his clothes before shows. She was a great friend of McQueen's right up until the end of his life and although a lot of attention is shone on McQueen's relationship with Isabella Blow, his friendship with Katy was one of love, quietness, a shared adoration and mutual creativity.

Sarah Burton was his design protégé. A quiet girl from northern England who grew up wearing her brother's hand-me-downs, she longed for beautiful clothes. After her tutor at Central Saint Martins saw her keen eye for research, she was recommended for a job as McQueen's assistant. 'It was like sculpture – I've never seen anything like it,' she told *Vogue* of his working process. 'In such a short space of time he did everything. Tailoring, evening-wear, dresses, embroidery, leather, knits – everything!'

Burton learned everything she knew working next to McQueen, by listening, observing and – in the early years – through never being able to make a mistake, because there was no money to remake something that had gone wrong. At McQueen's right hand for fourteen years, Burton was his trusted sidekick – and when it came to design, she could do anything he asked of her.

In 2000, McQueen got married. His homosexuality wasn't necessarily accepted by his family. When asked if his fame and fortune had changed their attitudes, he replied, 'No. They haven't always been cool about it. My father was a London taxi driver, and he would come home at night and say, "God I nearly ran over a bloody queer last night," and then all of a sudden everything's hunky dory just because I'm solvent? I can't buy that.'

Nonetheless, after a boozy night at the Groucho Club with Kate Moss, Annabelle Neilson and his boyfriend George Forsyth, he planned a wedding. It was before the UK legalised gay marriage. A few months after the engagement, McQueen and Forsyth flew to Ibiza and married among a star-studded throng aboard a three-storey yacht. It was the perfect setting for McQueen's only marriage, for his love of animals also extended to the sea and the creatures within it. Yet despite the fact that they were ferociously in love, the marriage lasted little over a year: the ferocity turned sour, and they made one another dreadfully unhappy.

In his later years McQueen would retire weekly to his cottage, a converted granary in East Sussex with views of the sea and – on a clear night – the sparkling lights of northern France. 'I don't find inspiration there – it gives me a peace of mind. Solitude, and a blank canvas to work from, instead of the distractions of the concrete jungle,' McQueen once said.

Although McQueen was achieving huge critical success, his business at its all-time peak and his income higher than ever, it all came to an end on the morning of 11 February 2010. At the age of forty, just three years after the tragic suicide of Isabella Blow and nine days after the death of his beloved mother, Joyce, Alexander McQueen took his own life.

While many in the fashion industry had been aware that McQueen struggled with depression, nobody expected such genius to end in such tragedy. That morning, his housekeeper arrived at McQueen's London home to find that the designer had hanged himself with his favourite brown belt. A post-mortem later announced that McQueen had imbibed a cocktail of drugs and slit his wrists with a meat cleaver and a ceremonial dagger. He left a single note, which read, 'Please look after my dogs. Sorry. I love you. Lee.'

The world was in shock, as was his family, who'd had no idea how severely unwell Lee had been. 'If we had known the extent of it, we would have been bashing down doors, but we didn't,' his sister Janet said. 'We all spoke to Lee about the drugs, but he was a man in his late thirties. I don't want to name names, I've got to be careful, but people knew his state of mind and his family didn't ... They knew about the other suicide attempts. We didn't.'

A few weeks later, at St Paul's Church in Knightsbridge, London, the high priests of fashion attended an incredibly sombre funeral for the man who had changed fashion, and the world. Along with his grieving family, Naomi Campbell, Kate Moss, Anna Wintour and Stella McCartney sent fashion's rebel king off to take his final bow. His legacy is perhaps the most influential the fashion world has ever witnessed. It is through his clothes, his ideas and his influence that he lives on – and will live on forever.

The
Collections

Chapter 6

2002–05

Times were changing once again for McQueen whose tenure at Givenchy had come to an end. He had taken Paris by storm, and cemented London on the global fashion map as a place to absolutely be taken seriously, both in terms of utter creativity and commercial dependability. Quite the achievement for someone in their early thirties. But as fashion was then, it had the power to give everything... and take it all away.

McQueen did not necessarily agree with the French house Givenchy. Today, those collections are looked back upon with great love and adoration, so it seems ironic and such a waste that the work he was creating – challenging, sexual, painful, and at times pushing the boundaries of what was deemed, then, good taste – can only be really appreciated posthumously. But that is the fickleness of fashion.

Lee was back to designing for his namesake label, between London and Paris. In 2001, he sold the majority share of his eponymous brand to fashion titans the Gucci group, yet retained full creative control. Now was time for expansion, as was the attitude in the early 2000s. First came a fragrance – the legendary 'Kingdom' in 2003, then 'My Queen' the following year. Next, his first menswear collection, for which the British Fashion Council awarded Lee 'Menswear Designer of the Year'.

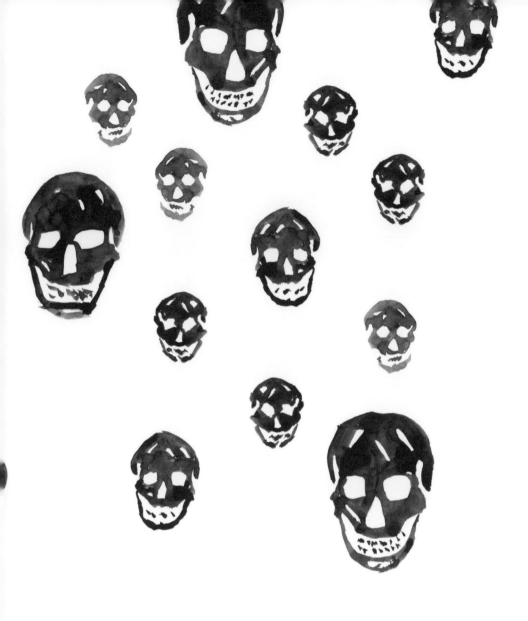

It was McQueen back at the helm of McQueen – and while the shows garnered mixed reviews, his creativity and vision never ceased. In 2003, he was awarded a CBE for his extraordinary contributions to British fashion and culture.

Concerned by the loss of industry in the UK, upon receiving his CBE McQueen said, 'I now formally urge the British Government to match this recognition by investing in manufacturing and new talent – the foundation of British Fashion.'

SPRING/SUMMER 2002
'The Dance of the Twisted Bull'

In Paris now, where he had just left his directorship at Givenchy, McQueen drew inspiration from Spanish flamenco dance and bull-fighting culture. The collection displayed a sort of exaggerated femininity, one of performance and passion – one that dices with danger. And yet this collection marked a turn in the tide for McQueen: yes, it was high concept, yes, it was dramatic, but it was notably less so than other collections under the eponymous label. McQueen had just sold his namesake label to the Gucci group, and he told the press that he wanted to focus on the design, bring in a new type of customer, in order to drive sales under this new ownership. And that it did: the collection reportedly flew off the shelves. Of course, one dress still courted controversy: the flamenco dancer pierced by two spears. It wouldn't be a McQueen show without a little drama!

AUTUMN/WINTER 2002

'Supercalifragilistic-expialidocious'

In Paris again, and hyper-focused on the clothes now, this was a collection with perhaps the least theatrics ever. A woman in a lavender cape stalked the runway with two huskies on a leash to open the show. And then after? Razor-sharp tailoring, a close eye on every detail. Brown tweed and braces, leather corsets and peasant necklines made for a collection that was 'about the women', as McQueen said. Body conscious, but in a way that worked with the models' bodies and not against them. Lace-up leather boots and denim skirts cut on the hoop, jeans on a Paris runway, and eventually beautiful buttery pink leathers and deep maroon pencil skirts. By now, the world knew that McQueen could bring drama to the runway, but he still liked to remind them that if there was something he was even better at than scandal it was making clothes.

SPRING/SUMMER 2003
'Irere'

Irere is an indigenous Amazonian word that means 'transformation', which was the theme for McQueen's twenty-first collection. From pirates to tropical birds, McQueen once again was less focused on the theatrics of the space and more focused on the clothes. That's not to say that there weren't flourishes of drama: the oyster dress became one of his most praised pieces of design, with thousands of oyster shapes made from chiffon making up the skirt portion of the dress. The shipwreck pirate dress is perhaps one of McQueen's better-known pieces, too. The response from the press was mixed: everyone loved the clothes, speaking of this as a collection where McQueen really showed off his developing skill; and yet those who had previously bemoaned his macabre show tactics seemed to miss them now they were gone. Fashion is a fickle thing.

AUTUMN/WINTER 2003
'Scanners'

X-ray scans of McQueen's own brain were sent out to the fashion crowd as show invitations. The set was a desolate, dystopian ice-scape, and a wind tunnel hung overhead above the audience: a bleak setting, an arresting proposition. But 2003's 'Scanners' became known as one of McQueen's most beautiful in terms of the clothes, perhaps highlighted even further by their juxtaposition to the set. Inspirations came from all over the world, a sort of representation of McQueen's nomadic lifestyle. From Japanese fabrics to Siberian furs, McQueen was drawing from everywhere, showcasing the breadth of his influences. The final scene of the show featured a model in a long silk kimono battling through hard winds. Those who were there spoke of it as breathtaking.

SPRING/SUMMER 2004
'Deliverance'

Rehearsing in London for two weeks prior, a dance company, choreographed by the genius Michael Clark, made their way to Paris to perform in McQueen's show. *Vogue* said that this offering of dancers, all moving to an adaptation of Sydney Pollack's film *They Shoot Horses, Don't They?*, breathed much-needed life and showmanship into a flat-lining Fashion Week. Trust McQueen. The dancing yes! And the clothes, too: Swarovski thigh-high boots, impeccable tailoring, tulle and denim – all in motion on dancers and muscled-up sailors. At the end, in a silver gown, the lead dancer feigned a faint in the centre of the show space, to be carried off by McQueen and Clark, designer and choreographer, to rapturous applause.

AUTUMN/WINTER 2004
'Pantheon ad Lucem'

Eyes were on McQueen again: he'd just delivered his highly dramatic dance number, and had not shown up for his interview to take over design on Saint Laurent's Rive Gauche collections. 'I need to be doing McQueen with my eyes shut,' he was later quoted saying. Critics had once again been at his door, claiming that he relied on dramatics and needed to focus on the clothes. So, once again, he listened and responded, bringing a flesh-tone collection to the runway. Silks, lambswool and a slippery latex-looking fabric in tones of peach, brown, silver and deep purple. Everything looked like a rebirth of sorts. And maybe that's what McQueen was having.

SPRING/SUMMER 2005
'It's Only a Game'

A game of chess, in fact. McQueen, back to theatrics (yes!) decided to stage his Spring/Summer collection on a human-size chess board, pitting his models against each other. The clothes took inspiration from all over the world. Initially, the show began with more down-to-earth, wearable pieces – think sundresses, blazers, belted jackets. But as the show continued, looks became more elaborate, drawing inspiration from Japanese clothing all the way to American football silhouettes. Each model, once they'd walked the runway, lined up to form a great chess board. One by one, they played human chess, the climax seeing the queens – Hana Soukupová and Gemma Ward – circling each other.

AUTUMN/WINTER 2005
'The Man Who Knew Too Much'

Fashion was changing. By now, it was a big money business, far removed from the world that had raised McQueen as a designer. Back then, it was warehouses, squat parties and The Big Show. And while it had its problems, perhaps it was this commerciality that was the reason McQueen left this show through the back door, without speaking to the press. Based on Hitchcock films from the sixties, once again McQueen took us back in time with nipped-in waists, large beehives and cat-eyed glamour. Criticism was brought against the middle part of the show where Navajo-print blankets and beige tasselled denims seemed to take over — *Vogue* calling it amusingly 'a merchandise run-through of dubious taste'. This balance is hard for any artist, the balance between commerciality and art, especially one as brilliant, as depended upon, and as scrutinised as Lee McQueen.

McQueen

Chapter 7

the Brand

From McQueen's first collection in 1992, which he sold in its entirety to Isabella Blow for £5000, to his multimillion-dollar global fashion house, his eponymous brand, Alexander McQueen, has always been lauded and coveted. McQueen's creativity was big business – he produced breathtaking collections of impeccably made, incredibly wearable clothes that women and men wanted to buy. He was known for his signature theatrics and showmanship, and revered for his flawless tailoring, daring cuts and exquisite use of fabrics. At its core today, years after McQueen's death, the brand remains true to its founder's ultimate vision: to offer women the chance to dress powerfully and beautifully.

Fashion is nothing without its wearers. A controversial opinion, and one vehemently opposed by fashion aesthetes, is that it doesn't matter how artistic a collection might be – if it doesn't sell, there will be no money to make the next collection. It's no surprise, then, that many designers focus on creating clothes that are sellable, living radiantly glamorous, all-expenses-paid lives with little artistic integrity. Other designers, who commit solely to art, often find themselves under serious financial strain, forced to abandon their fashion dreams for more profitable pursuits. But not McQueen.

'I came to terms with not fitting in a long time ago. I never really fitted in. I don't want to fit in. And now people are buying into that.'

ALEXANDER MCQUEEN

McQueen was art, McQueen was the highest of high fashion. McQueen used his boundless creativity to make utterly fantastic, brilliantly beautiful and incredibly wearable clothes – clothes people wanted to buy. In his brand, he perfectly balanced art and commerce in a way no other brand had.

From its founding days in the early nineties, the Alexander McQueen brand quickly earned a reputation for its controversial approach to women's fashion, sparking countless cases of genuine outrage across the fashion community. Before long, McQueen had become known for his creative and daring approach to dressing women. He once described women wearing McQueen as 'women to be scared of'.

Lee was dubbed *'l'enfant terrible'*, 'the hooligan of British fashion'. Yet the brand was splashed across magazines and worn by the coolest editors, its shows walked and attended by the *crème de la crème* of fashion. It was the perfect foundation for any fashion label: daring, controversial, outrageous and beautiful.

While it took years, past the shocking 'Taxi Driver' and 'Highland Rape' collections, the fashion industry eventually saw beyond the showmanship and began to appreciate the clothes themselves. But McQueen continued to court controversy, always pushing the boundaries of what the fashion industry deemed acceptable. In 1998, he cast double amputee Aimee Mullins to walk down the runway on intricately carved wooden legs. The fashion industry called it disempowering, but Mullins and McQueen were proud to have platformed a model with a disability, saying that she had just as much right to a place on the runway as anyone else.

In 1999, the beautiful Shalom Harlow walked onto a rotating platform wearing a giant white dress. Two robotic arms on either side of the platform then sprayed the dress in neon yellow and black lines while an emotional audience watched. Katy England, McQueen's right-hand woman, said that this moment was the only time she ever saw McQueen moved to tears during one of his own shows. It has been described as one of the most profound moments in fashion history, capturing the interplay of aggression and vulnerability, exploring the relationship between our control over technology, and its control over us. The press couldn't decide if it was misogyny or genius.

Season upon season the brand's profile expanded, and the world's excitement skyrocketed. Fashion had never seen anything like it.

The hype around the brand, and McQueen himself, grew as the designer began to win fashion's highest awards. All through the nineties you could only buy a McQueen piece at selected boutiques and department stores, and the lone McQueen shop in London's West End. These stores became destinations, attracting flocks of shoppers from around the world desperate to snag a piece from *l'enfant terrible* of British fashion.

In December 2000, the Gucci group – under the direction of the lauded designer Tom Ford, who had been a big inspiration for McQueen – bought 51 per cent of the brand and appointed Lee as creative director. This meant that Lee, who continued to own 49 per cent of the brand, also kept complete creative control.

This huge, exciting investment saw him terminated from his post at Givenchy, a year before his contract with the fashion house was over. Now he could put all his energies into his eponymous label. After the deal was signed, flagship stores quickly opened across Europe and the United States: in London, Milan, New York, Los Angeles and Las Vegas. Now the brand had spread across the world, and fans could see the clothes they'd adored on the catwalk up close in store. And in true fashion style, under the guidance of the giant Gucci group, McQueen's shows relocated from London to Paris – the fashion capital of the world – premiering with the 2001 show 'The Dance of the Twisted Bull'.

This working-class lad made fashion exciting – daring – again. People wanted in. He had achieved the seemingly impossible: he'd mounted the fashion horse and charged the industry, rising as its king. He democratised fashion, demolishing its elitist walls, which sent a thrilling message to the world, to the people who loved fashion but never thought they'd get a look-in. McQueen had proven it could be done, and more and more people flocked to join the industry, which was growing at an unprecedented rate. McQueen had a huge hand in this expansion, too.

There was eyewear, fragrance, a diffusion line, menswear, womenswear, pre-fall and high-summer collections, make-up, handbags, accessories, and countless stores across the world. This was what global fashion domination looked like, and it was orchestrated masterfully by McQueen.

Alexander McQueen, as both a designer and a brand, fundamentally changed the fashion world. He blurred the lines between politics, art and clothes; manipulated the worldwide press; and boldly embraced technology. He always had his finger on the pulse. Anything the great designer threw at the world would stick, including his other brand collaborations with Samsonite, PUMA and Target.

Beyond his creations, which are a rich, complicated gift to fashion, art and culture, McQueen's brand lives on, continuing to dominate the fashion stage, a brilliant model for other designers the world over. Even after his death, the fashion industry continues to look to him for inspiration.

'I want to empower women. I want people to be scared of the women I dress.'

ALEXANDER MCQUEEN

THE FRAGRANCES

In January 2003, the noted perfumer Jacques Cavallier approached McQueen about collaborating on a fragrance. The brand's first scent, 'Kingdom', was launched on 17 March the same year – the day of McQueen's birthday. *Vogue* described it as 'a musky-oriental so heavy on the cumin that some hours after spraying, you could mistake it for body odour'. But of course a McQueen fragrance would never be gentle: even in making a fragrance he was disruptive.

THE SKULL SCARF

In the same year, as part of his 'Irere' collection, McQueen launched perhaps the most iconic of all of his brand symbols: the skull scarf. Copied the world over, and emulated by countless other designers, this became perhaps the world's most coveted, most well-worn accessory.

THE MENSWEAR COLLECTION

McQueen was in hot demand. In response to a growing global interest in men's fashion, he designed his first menswear collection in 2005 to critical, and commercial, acclaim. McQueen was known for his tailoring, and his ability to surprise, to challenge. He'd more than proven his mettle in the world of womenswear, so when he looked to desert troopers and military tailoring for his first menswear collection – yes, those two overused reference points in menswear design – McQueen made it work. Beautiful yellow tones, moss greens, cross-body harnesses. This was the beginning of menswear for the house, which continues to this day.

THE COSMETICS

In 2007, McQueen was the first designer to collaborate with the iconic make-up brand MAC Cosmetics, launching their premier collection of designer make-up. The collection took inspiration from McQueen's Autumn/Winter 2007 collection 'In Memory of Elizabeth Howe, Salem, 1692', where the models wore zany greens and teals on their eyes with strong slicks of black eyeliner, an homage to Elizabeth Taylor in the elaborate movie *Cleopatra* – long before the years of YouTube tutorials and *RuPaul's Drag Race*. As ever, McQueen was driving fashion into new arenas.

THE MCQ LINE

By 2008 the brand had grown so popular that it made sense for McQueen to launch a second, more affordable line: McQ, which has stores all over the world today. Originally touted as a denim line, the idea was to take the rebellious heart of the Alexander McQueen brand and channel it into more wearable, everyday pieces for his younger, more relaxed fans.

MCQUEEN ONLINE

In the same year, he took Alexander McQueen online in the US, adopting the digital shopping trend long before many other well-established design houses. McQueen had global reach, and the world was hooked.

The Collections

Chapter 8

2006–10

Business was booming at Alexander McQueen HQ, under the commercial leadership of the Gucci group. These years saw the launch of Pre-Fall and Cruise collections, the launch of the much-loved diffusion line, McQ, which offered a lower price point for fans of McQueen who wanted a piece of the designer but couldn't afford the super-high-fashion price tag. Having opened his London flagship in 2003, it was in the years between 2005 and 2010 that McQueen opened stores in Milan, New York and Los Angeles (at the time of writing, the brand has over 100 stores worldwide).

And while everything seemed smooth sailing on the business side, in the mid-2000s McQueen had called foul on the fashion critics who loved him so much. The general feeling seemed to be that he was failing to find that sweet spot between art and commerce – his collections seeming more business-bent. Of course, McQueen being McQueen he soon made his creative comeback, first with his legendary 2006 collection 'The Widows of Culloden', which saw Kate Moss appear as a hologram, and then with one of his most critically acclaimed works, 'Sarabande', in 2007.

Soon after his return to form in every sense, McQueen would
lose his first and most fierce mentor, Isabella Blow. He went
on to say that her death was 'the most valuable thing I learnt in
fashion'. The spectre of death would continue to plague McQueen
and a few years later he also lost his beloved mother. On the day
before her funeral, in February 2010, McQueen took his own life.

SPRING/SUMMER 2006
'Neptune'

McQueen's star continued to fall among the fashion critics, who expected more of him than his twenty-seventh collection 'Neptune' offered. Featuring a lot of black, boxy outfits, many saw this as a loss of McQueen's trademark finesse when it came to tailoring. Of course, others disagreed, rather loving this step towards a more modern, less typically feminine woman when it came to tailoring. Fast-forward twenty looks and the part of the show inspired by Greek goddesses came: silver cut-out bikinis made from what appeared to be metal, and long, flowing Grecian gowns with large warrior-like belts. Yet, all in all, Neptune didn't quite rise, it seemed – the most memorable image from the collection being one of the designer during his bow, where he appeared in a T-shirt that read 'We Love You Kate' after she had been caught up in a recent media scandal.

AUTUMN/WINTER 2006
'The Widows of Culloden'

Revisiting his Scottish heritage after the outrageous, much-acclaimed 'Highland Rape' of the early nineties, this show demonstrated McQueen's huge growth as a designer. 'The Widows of Culloden' explored Pre-Raphaelite visions of women wandering glens, and a more punkish plaid dress with armour instead of sleeves, all produced with a honed technical ability that resulted in beautiful dresses and sharp tweed suits. The beginning of the show was McQueen's first real foray into technology, with a glass pyramid bringing to life a dancing, floating Kate Moss in the form of a hologram. The audience were silenced as she floated through virtual and physical space in a windblown white Victoriana-style dress, only to disappear in a puff of white smoke.

'There's something sinister and romantic about clothes, and I've always felt like a spy.'

ALEXANDER MCQUEEN

SPRING/SUMMER 2007
'Sarabande'

McQueen was back! After the long-reigning tension between art and commerce, with 'Sarabande' – a show to this day many say was one of his greatest in terms of the clothes – McQueen managed to hush the critics. He went back to his own work, and to Goya (of course), and what came forth was sharp tailoring around his beloved Edwardian-leaning silhouette of the nipped-in waist. He showed everything: dresses, tunics, bridal, grey trousers, all – or most – of it in some sort of close relationship with laces, tulles and chiffons. Structure met softness, full coverage from suiting was broken with sheers, almost translucent, under blouses. By the end of the show, proportions were exaggerated – hips stuffed with flowers, a crumb-catching corset overflowing with blooms, too. Bravo!

AUTUMN/WINTER 2007
'In Memory of Elizabeth Howe, Salem, 1692'

McQueen was inspired by his own family history for Autumn/ Winter 2007. After his mother, who had been researching their family tree, had discovered they were descended from Elizabeth Howe, a far-off relative who had been falsely accused of witchcraft and hanged in the 1692 Salem Witch Trials, McQueen drew from the imagery, symbolism and clothing of different persecuted peoples across history. In the centre of the show space hung a 50-foot inverted black pyramid, which became a screen depicting a self-directed film of bodies and locusts, above a blood-red pentagram that the models walked on. And while the whole show was super theatrical, the clothes were surprisingly accessible: black or beige body-conscious dresses nipped in at the waist and exaggerated at the shoulder; golds and purples with tailored elements (of course), and a heavy use of Egyptian-style golds. The more show-stopping pieces were bodices formed to the body from leather and metal.

SPRING/SUMMER 2008
'La Dame Bleue'

The late Isabella Blow became McQueen's muse for this collection, which was shown in Paris and dedicated to her memory. It was a deeply moving collection, designed in collaboration with Blow's other protégé, Philip Treacy. McQueen's previous collection had famously been poorly received, but – perhaps for Issie – this time, he was back on form with bulging hip jackets, fairy-like chiffon dresses and a rainbow-winged gown. It was glorious and full of movement and emotion: the very qualities Issie had always championed, and celebrated, in McQueen.

AUTUMN/WINTER 2008
'The Girl Who Lived in the Tree'

McQueen had a 600-year-old elm tree in his back garden, and he'd made up this story about a girl who descends from living in the tree to marry a prince, thus becoming a queen. This was 'The Girl Who Lived in the Tree', and she was dressed in some of McQueen's most stunning clothes. The critics raved about this as one of McQueen's most breathtaking, most beautiful collections ever. He had been so inspired after a trip to India that he apparently spent night and day in his studio conceptualising and designing the collection. A riff on, and critique of, British colonialism in India, McQueen dressed his models in absurd diamonds and jewels, ermines and velvets, which became more voluminous as the show went on. From the tree to the throne, the girl was both swamped and in full colour.

SPRING/SUMMER 2009
'Natural Dis-tinction, Un-natural Selection'

In a previous life the show space for S/S '09 had been a morgue, and the runway was filled with antique taxidermy – from a polar bear to ostriches, peacocks and zebras. It was a spectacle to say the least, and McQueen's reference to evolution, to Darwinism, and to the brutality of both nature and industry. And to its beauty. The clothes reflected this, too: armour-like dresses, which glistened, were exaggerated at the hip, while necklines dove down to the navel. Beautiful, breathtaking dresses in white silk, just like clouds, were cinched beyond belief by leather waspies, like the carapaces of hard-shelled animals. It was a moment, a step into real future-bent aesthetics from a designer who had been looking back a lot in previous collections. To top it off, he took his bow in a giant bunny costume.

AUTUMN/WINTER 2009
'The Horn of Plenty'

Once again a controversy, but fashion loves (and hates!) the charade of it all. By 2009, people were growing in frustration with the seeming idea that fashion was now sheerly about business. And so McQueen put on a show. Broken and discarded parts of sets from his own shows framed a broken glass runway, and the collection was almost parodic – blow-up-doll versions of legendary fashion looks from the past. The Dior New Look in a huge houndstooth, a Chanel jacket, and even some of Lee's biggest hitters made their way back to the runway. It was showmanship at its best, even if the critics didn't think the clothes were his best.

SPRING/SUMMER 2010
'Plato's Atlantis'

By this time McQueen had become the world's fashion icon – and Lady Gaga's, too. 'Plato's Atlantis' is perhaps one of McQueen's most deified collections: one that fearlessly embraced new technologies that the rest of the fashion industry was perhaps too timid to face head-on. On the day of the show Lady Gaga tweeted that she would be premiering her brand-new single during McQueen's runway show, which fans all over the world could witness by tuning in to a livestream on Nick Knight's groundbreaking website SHOWstudio.

People went online to watch fashion history in motion, prompting so many logins that the site crashed. But the show, as ever, had to go on. What was shown was an amalgam of influences: fish and butterfly prints, drawn from McQueen's adoration of scuba diving, were printed onto stiff fabrics that were nipped and tucked into bulbous tulip skirts and wrapped tightly around torsos. The models became anthropomorphised versions of tropical fish and coral reefs, a thematic evolution for McQueen that dissected humankind's evolution from the seas. Cameras on sliding runners filmed the audience's reaction and projected it onto massive screens that flanked the entrance of the runway. The result was to make the fashion crowd stare at themselves, a favourite trick of the designer's. This show saw the birth of McQueen's genius armadillo boots, as well as the start of fashion's ever-evolving relationship with technology.

AUTUMN/WINTER 2010
'Angels and Demons'

McQueen's suicide in 2010 came just before he was due to present his latest collection, 'Angels and Demons', in Paris. McQueen had left a lasting legacy on the fashion industry, and the wider world, showing artists of all kinds the creative and political potential and influence one person can have. Left behind, too, was a small, delicate collection of sixteen pieces, which would be shown in a small salon in Paris, shared with friends from both within fashion and outside it. For his final-ever collection, McQueen looked back: back into beauty, fine craftsmanship and his own archives. Each dress was draped on a mannequin and had been cut, sewn and pressed by McQueen. Eschewing his prior interest in technology in favour of iconic religious women – whose figures were sewn into the fabrics – McQueen's little-known posthumous collection was a powerful, emotional look at the things he loved best: craft, skill, elegance, tailoring, darkness and light, and – of course – the women whom he dressed. It was tailoring in all its precision, and romanticism in all its beauty and freedom.

The
Legacy

Chapter 9

When McQueen died, he left behind a fashion industry that was completely different from the one he had entered. He not only built a multimillion-dollar global brand and an extensive and impressive oeuvre, he also created a new silhouette, revolutionised the idea of a runway show and its audience, and changed the way women dressed. He re-imagined what fashion could be, what it could mean – as fashion, as art, as political comment. But perhaps his most important legacy was that he used the power of fashion to democratise dreams and to challenge how we think and how we live.

From Kate Middleton's (now Catherine, Princess of Wales) royal wedding dress to a smash-hit retrospective exhibition, McQueen's ideas live on. His brand thrives and his influence can still be seen on runways, in fashion magazines, in lecture halls and in art.

His legacy fulfilled his wishes perfectly: in fashion, everyone knows that the 21st century was started by Alexander McQueen. Fashion is a world that looks in on itself, and it is undoubtable that the fashion masterpieces created by McQueen will be referenced, adored and celebrated for decades to come.

'When I'm dead and gone, people will know that the 21st century was started by Alexander McQueen.'

ALEXANDER MCQUEEN

But McQueen's legacy is more than just his fashion. After his tragic death, Alexander McQueen left £50,000 of his £16-million fortune to his dogs to ensure that they would be pampered for the rest of their lives. He left £250,000 to each of his siblings, £50,000 each to his godson, nieces and nephews, and long-time housekeepers.

The rest of his estate went to charities. Two of these were dedicated to caring for dogs, another was the Terrence Higgins Trust – an important HIV and AIDS charity in the UK. McQueen also set up a trust fund named the Sarabande Trust, which shares a name with his Spring/Summer 2007 collection. He asked that the trust be used to offer bursaries or grants to students from working-class backgrounds to help them secure a place at university, studying in the creative arts. Although McQueen had by then become accustomed to the luxuries his success afforded him, he hadn't forgotten his beginnings. When he gained his place at Central Saint Martins, if his aunt hadn't lent him the £4000 course fee, the world may never have witnessed the genius of McQueen.

THE HIPSTER

Beyond his estate, McQueen also left enduring imprints on many parts of the fashion industry, as well as wider culture. McQueen invented, and championed, the low-slung jean silhouette. After he invented the Bumster – estimated to be owned by no more than twenty people in the UK, with a pair selling at auction for a mighty £3500 – the trend of elongating the body by exposing the midriff swept high fashion, as well as the high street, and continues to feature strongly in fashion today as the hipster.

A DARKER SIDE OF FASHION

McQueen's exploration of death, darkness and the macabre created collections and clothing that resonated emotionally with people both inside and outside of the fashion industry. Perhaps the most worn piece of McQueen's oeuvre is the skull scarf, which has inspired numerous designers and spawned countless counterfeits over the years. Journalist and fashion critic Suzy Menkes once said, 'There was something inside his head and his mind that you didn't want to know about.' While that was true for some, the darkness McQueen expressed across his body of work resonated with many, and also inspired whole movements in music, art and fashion.

WOMEN AS PREDATORS

McQueen graduated from his years on Savile Row with an expert knowledge of cutting and tailoring, which he brought to women's clothing. By reinterpreting classically male codes of dress, introducing severe cutting to his designs, he repositioned the way many women dressed. Although he was often criticised for these designs – with people calling collections such as 'Highland Rape' misogynistic – many people felt he was actually exploring women as predators, as strong people to be reckoned with. 'They don't look vulnerable,' Professor Claire Wilcox, senior curator of fashion at the Victoria and Albert Museum, once said. 'Actually, they look like they might punch you.'

McQueen often said he was designing armour, and his references always cited strong, persecuted women from history, such as his collection 'Joan', inspired by Joan of Arc, as well as Pope Joan.

It was a new move in fashion, one that hadn't been as central to womenswear since Yves Saint Laurent had put his models in suits back in 1966. McQueen surrounded himself with strong women, including his right-hand woman, Katy England, his muse and biggest supporter, Isabella Blow, and his mother, Joyce, whom he adored.

NEW BOUNDARIES FOR BEAUTY

McQueen loved to profile and platform 'unconventional' models. From double amputee Aimee Mullins to performance artist Michelle Olley, who appeared naked as the centrepiece for his controversial 'Voss' show, and who carried significantly more weight than the usual size-zero fashion model. After agreeing to do the show, which has since become one of fashion's most celebrated visuals, Olley wrote the following in her diary:

So, diary, why am I doing this? It's not for fashion. I couldn't give a monkey's purple bum about fashion. It's not my friend, denying me access through its gates with bitey little zips, unbending waist measurements and impossible standards. I'm not scared of looking ugly, but public nudity is really not my bag. Why, when McQueen was explaining it, was one half of me screaming 'Yes!' while the other was going 'Arrrrgh – scary!'?

As scary as it was, McQueen was forever asking his muses to put themselves in different and difficult situations in order to express another side of fashion, of beauty, of life. His fascination with the female form, and with new ways of draping clothes upon it, as well as the symbolism that informed his designs – from Victoriana, to witchcraft, to paganism, to religion, to sex – meant that McQueen made countless things that were deemed ugly by society totally and utterly beautiful.

FASHION AS THEATRE AND POLITICS

McQueen entered the ring and significantly changed the world's attitude to fashion, and to what could be in fashion. Through his shows he discussed provocative topics such as mental illness, decay and death, disability, menstruation, vivisection, and the primal nature of humanity. The heralded designer paid homage to the women he designed for by dedicating his life to creating the most beautiful, sensational clothes for them to wear.

McQueen also pioneered fashion's theatrical potential: before him, fashion shows had never been quite so extravagant, visually stimulating or theatrically moving. McQueen built entirely new sets, he added countless new dimensions to the way fashion shows could be presented, he moved audiences to tears and outrage, and ultimately used fashion as a means of provocation. Not only did McQueen introduce many new things into fashion, he ingrained them into its nature, raising people's expectations of fashion as a whole, and leaving it as so much more than it had been when he entered.

AND ULTIMATELY, SAVAGE BEAUTY

In May 2011, the Metropolitan Museum of Art in New York opened the doors to one of its most successful exhibitions ever. *Savage Beauty*, curated by Andrew Bolton and Harold Koda, displayed the late Alexander McQueen's archive for the world to see. And see it, they did – first via video and imagery taken after fashion's biggest event, the Met Gala, organised by *Vogue* editor Anna Wintour, and then in reality by people who flocked in droves – a staggering 650,000 over three months – to see the life's work of one of fashion's most groundbreaking designers.

The exhibition comprised a comprehensive look through the archives of McQueen's own brand, and also featured pieces from the designer's tenure at Givenchy. It was arranged in six different galleries, each of which tethered multiple collections together in one theme. 'The Romantic Mind' featured McQueen's earlier, more poetic work. 'Romantic Gothic and the Cabinet of Curiosities' focused on McQueen's obsession with all things Victoriana: housed in a giant room across endless shelves and boxes, it featured some of McQueen's most imaginative pieces, from dresses, to jewellery, to headpieces. 'Romantic Nationalism' examined McQueen's exploration of his British and Scottish identity, profiling his finest tailoring and pieces from the controversial, iconic 'Highland Rape' collection – the collection that arguably put McQueen on the map. 'Romantic Exoticism' deconstructed his view of non-western influences, while 'Romantic Primitivism' featured natural materials and organic designs. The journey ended with 'Romantic Naturalism', analysing McQueen's attempts to integrate fashion, evolution, nature and technology.

Viewers looked on in awe, aware it was perhaps the only time they would get to see pieces from 'Jack the Ripper Stalks His Victims', 'Voss', 'Irere' and 'Plato's Atlantis', as well as the mind-blowing life-sized hologram of Kate Moss that featured in his romantic collection, 'The Widows of Culloden'. The exhibition set out to leave people feeling uneasy, and it did. Viewers were plunged into the mind of a man who was plagued with genius and darkness in equal measure.

The popularity of *Savage Beauty* saw it subsequently shown in London, from March to August 2015. Housed in the great Victoria and Albert Museum, *Savage Beauty* remains the museum's highest selling show to date, drawing over half a million people through its doors. It was the first time the museum had ever extended its opening hours, and in the final weeks of the show the exhibit stayed open twenty-four hours a day to meet the demand of those anxious to witness the legacy of London's most lauded designer.

But it is impossible to measure a person's legacy through the material things they leave behind. McQueen changed fashion, he altered the way both women and men dress, and he established an influential and groundbreaking brand that continued to thrive in the hands of its successive creative director Sarah Burton, who celebrated the legacy of McQueen the best way she knew how: with precision focus on the tailoring, the cuts, the fabrics. That was her role when Lee was alive, and it continued after his passing. At the end of 2023, on exiting her role, people paid their respects to Sarah, saying that she had revolutionised the way women dress, and are allowed to think about dressing, today. Seán McGirr is next to take up the mantle as creative director.

Most of all, however, McQueen left behind proof that creativity and imagination can capture the minds of so many, and that things in our dreams can become reality. He inspired countless people to enter not only the fashion industry, but also the creative arts more widely. His clothes empowered their wearers. While tragic, McQueen's battle with depression and his eventual suicide stoked the conversation around mental health in the creative arts.

McQueen, both in life and in death, was a renegade, a legend, a true genius and, perhaps most importantly, a person who set out to do something and did it, with passion, vigour and tenacity.

'Some designers are so airy-fairy people can't connect with them. I hope that people can relate to me, to a normal person who just happens to be a fashion designer, that people can take me as they find me.'

ALEXANDER MCQUEEN

Index

Published in 2024 by
Smith Street Books
Naarm (Melbourne) | Australia
smithstreetbooks.com

ISBN: 978-1-9230-4953-6

Smith Street Books respectfully
acknowledges the Wurundjeri
People of the Kulin Nation, who
are the Traditional Owners of the
land on which we work, and we pay
our respects to their Elders past
and present.

Publisher: Hannah Koelmeyer
Editor: Emily Preece-Morrison
Design & layout: Francesca Corsini
Illustrations: Angie Réhe
Proofreader: Pam Dunne
Indexer: Helena Holmgren

Printed & bound in China by C&C
Offset Printing Co., Ltd.

Book 347
10 9 8 7 6 5 4 3 2 1

MIX
Paper | Supporting
responsible forestry
FSC® C008047